C000016004

IMAGES OF ENGLAND

Around Camberley

IMAGES OF ENGLAND

Around Camberley

Ken Clarke

NONSUCH

First published 1995
This new pocket edition 2005
Images unchanged from first edition

Nonsuch Publishing Limited
The Mill, Brimscombe Port,
Stroud, Gloucestershire, GL5 2QG
www.nonsuch-publishing.com

British Library Cataloguing in Publication Data.
A catalogue record for this book is available from the British Library.

ISBN 1-84588-135-4

Typesetting and origination by Nonsuch Publishing Limited
Printed in Great Britain by Oaklands Book Services Limited

Contents

Acknowledgements

Thanks go to Colin Sinnott and Dusty Miller who both kindly allowed me to borrow from their collections of photographs and postcards. I would also like to thank John Sparks for the picture of The Jolly Farmer on page 25, and Fred Smith for the photo of Kate Ward on page 98.

It has been said that although God cannot alter the past, historians can, it is perhaps because they can be useful to Him in this respect that He tolerates their existence.

Samuel Butler, 1835–1902

Introduction

This essentially Victorian Town owes its existence to the decision to build the Royal Military College here at the beginning of the nineteenth century. At that time there were only a few people living in the area, the population in 1811 numbering 702.

In the eighteenth century, the area was described as barren, and those who travelled on its roads not only had to endure the rigours of a mail coach and the tracks through the forests, but also ran the risk of being held up by the numerous highwaymen who plied their trade on the infamous 'Bagshot Heath'. The most famous of these was William Davis, who was more commonly known as the Golden Farmer due to the fact that he paid all his debts in gold which he had obtained from his secondary occupation. Others of the same fraternity included the Frenchman Claude du Vall, Thomas Simpson, and Whitney the Butcher. They all ended their days at the end of the hangman's noose, but not before becoming part of the history of the area.

The town had started to grow and New Town, subsequently changing its name to York Town, was built to accommodate the newcomers. Fifty years later the Staff College was completed, and Cambridge Town was built. It was not until 1877, owing to confusion with Cambridge in Cambridgeshire and mail being misdirected, that the decision was made to change the name of Cambridge Town to Camberley.

With the arrival of the railway from Ascot the following year and owing to the fact that the pine-tree hills of the area were thought to be beneficial to sufferers from tuberculosis, the town's expansion commenced. By the turn of the century there were more than 8,400 residents and it was fast becoming the 'in place' to live. It was most popular with those retiring from army life who were seeking a place to retreat to. A quote from one army magazine extols the virtues of the area: 'For miles around there stretches a glorious expanse of hilly country partly covered with pines, partly consisting of gorse and heather clad common. It is impossible to exhaust the charms of the scenery which unfold in every direction.' Could this be the same area referred to by William Cobbett in 1830 in his book *Rural Rides?* 'Great numbers have seen the wide sweep of barrenness which exhibits itself between the Golden Farmer [now the Jolly Farmer] and Blackwater.'

The R.M.C. and the Staff College grounds were open for all to enjoy and the Army played their part in the social activities of the Town. Then the First World War took its toll and 233 young men of the town never returned. A further 140 were lost in the Second World War.

With the coming of the Old Dean Estate in the 1950s and the building of the factory estate in York Town, Camberley grew at a fast rate and by 1961 the population was 28,552. At the end of the 1960s it was decided to build a town centre and this meant the destruction of the heart of the town. Many older properties were demolished and much of the Victorian atmosphere disappeared. Even more old buildings have gone since this time.

This quiet residential town has seen many changes and is now the focal point of a much wider area, Surrey Heath, having changed from the old Frimley and Camberley Urban District Council, which was formed in 1929. The tarmacadam roads used to be dusty tracks, and the once-familiar sound of horses' hooves has all but gone. This primarily military town, with its large country houses with maids and servants, has changed. Most of these large houses have now been replaced with small neat houses, and the once common sight of boys delivering goods to one's door has disappeared. These old pictures provide a good insight into how Camberley used to be, and show a quiet respectable town where life was orderly and more disciplined than it is today. The quiet tranquillity has been replaced by a bustling area of shopping and a vibrant town.

I did not become interested in history until some fifteen years ago after many talks with my late father, who was always telling me what Camberley was like when he was young. This started me thinking that if no one wrote about it then in a few years this history would be lost. Some thirteen books later I am still an avid historian, and still enjoy looking at old pictures and photos of the town and surrounding area.

I hope that after reading this book you too will have gained some pleasure from looking at the 'old days', and perhaps can imagine how people looked and lived in this town of ours, when things were a lot different.

One

Camberley
(Cambridge Town)

In my time the follies of the town crept slowly among us,
but now they travel faster than a stagecoach.

Oliver Goldsmith, 1728–1774

This 1979 picture shows what is left of the obelisk situated on the knoll behind the Surrey Heath Offices. It was originally built about 1750 by John Norris, who lived in Hawley, to communicate with his friends the Dashwoods of West Wycombe. It used to consist of four arches with a gold ball on top, surrounded by a balcony. There are many names carved very deep into the brickwork, and enquiries show that most of these names were carved by officer cadets from the Military College who walked up the knoll. Obelisk Street, now Obelisk Way, was named after this monument.

High Street, 1910, with Sadler and Bakers Estate Agents next door to the old Police Station, surrounded by a brick wall. Sergeant Kenward lived at the Station and had eight Constables to patrol the Town. Drake and Mounts, coal, corn and forage merchants' shop, is on the left.

A 1908 look at High Street, at the junction of St George's Road and Obelisk Street. Evans is now the Halifax Building Society.

London Road *c.* 1915, with Darracott's vehicle outside the Cambridge Hotel at the High Street junction. Built in 1862, the hotel was named after the Duke of Cambridge, who was at one time the Commander-in-Chief of the British Army.

This postcard is dated 1906, and shows the High Street looking towards the Station. The lady who wrote the card has marked where she was staying at the time. Sworders electrical shop is on the right.

London Road and High Street in 1970, with a Cambridge Hotel which has changed since the picture opposite was taken. Whites petrol station, with the clock above, can be seen on the right, on the corner of Knoll Road. The large window of the hotel, seen in the High Street, was part of the Cambridge Tea Rooms, a very select place to have one's tea. In 2004 it changed hands again, and is now called the RSVP, but I am hoping that in the near future it will be rebranded The Cambridge Hotel.

Brackendale Road in 1912, showing the pine trees for which Camberley was well known at the time. The area was developed from 1895 onwards.

Tekels Avenue, c. 1930. This road was named after John Tekell who at one time lived in Frimley Park, which is now owned by the army and is opposite Do-It-All in the Frimley Road.

High Street and London Road in 1943, with the National Westminster Bank on the far corner of the High Street. On the back of the post card is printed 'TNT' – Today Not Tomorrow.

A scene from about 1910 of the London Road, with the Cambridge Hotel in the distance on the right. The second shop on the right is Sparvells the bakers and grocers. Mr Sparvell became an Alderman and has a walk named after him in the town centre.

London Road, *c.* 1906, with the London and Provincial Bank being the first shop. Next door is the Post Office run by Mr Norman, who from 1890–1920 was the first postmaster in Camberley.

The signpost on the right indicates the way to Camberley Station and points to the High Street in this 1926 photo. Traffic lights were not yet necessary at this junction.

A 1926 view of the London Road looking towards Blackwater with the old Post Office on the left. The top of St Tarcisius' Church can be seen just beyond the next building. The war memorial on the right was erected in 1922 and now commemorates all those who perished in both wars, 233 in the First World War, and 140 in the Second World War. It cost about £433.

In 1905 the London Road, with Park Street to the left, looked very quiet. Beyond is the sign for the Staff Hotel. Opposite is the Staff College entrance.

Camberley, King's Ride.

King's Ride at its junction with London Road in 1913. It was so named because King George III used the track as a short cut to Windsor Castle.

An early view of London Road c. 1905, with the Cambridge Hotel the last building on the right.

GREETINGS FROM

ENTRANCE TO SANDHURST, MILITARY ACADEMY.

KINGS WALK, ROYAL MILITARY ACADEMY

CHURCH OF ST. MICHAEL & ST. GEORGE.

CAMBERLEY

HIGH STREET.

C.BY 31   Copyright T. Sergeant

LONDON ROAD.

A 1953 greetings card extolling the virtues of Camberley.

London Road looking towards the Cambridge Hotel in 1917. The optician's shop of
V. Cunningham is the first shop on the right. He joined the Artists' Rifles and sadly lost his life
during the First World War, on 30 October 1917, after being wounded at Passchendaele.

This is the house where, on 11 June 1906, Mary Anne Hogg was murdered. The house was called Heathfield and was in the London Road opposite Diamond Ridge. It has since been demolished. She lived there with her half sister, Caroline Gwinnell Hogg; they were both rather eccentric in their habits and used to wear old-fashioned clothes. Mary Anne was discovered in the hallway of the house with her throat cut. The inquest was adjourned several times but the police never caught the culprit and the case is still classed as outstanding. The postcard is dated 14 July 1906.

These are the grounds of a house called Dullatur, which was next door but one to Heathfield, where Miss Hogg was murdered, and it was through these gardens that Caroline ran before shouting to the occupant, 'I'm murdered, I'm murdered'. The occupants, Mrs Wilding and her daughter, arranged for a doctor and the police to attend.

Judging by the long shadows, this early 1900 view of Church Hill was taken on a very sunny day.

A very picturesque photo of Camberley Court Hotel, formerly a house called Firlands House, which was at the junction of Park Road and Firlands Avenue. In the 1930s it was described as 'The finest residential hotel in the district'.

Kingsclear, Park Road, c. 1955. Now a retirement home, when it was built in about 1890 it was home to Mr Charles C. King, who named it Kingsclere.

It's 1935, and here we see Tim, who was well known by most of the shopkeepers in Camberley as he and his driver, Harry Gould, were responsible for the delivery of the parcels and packages that arrived at the Railway Station. Tim was stabled at the Railway Station and he and Harry were together for sixteen years. He is seen here having his regular bun from the cafe in the station yard and bus station, now part of Pembroke Broadway. One year he achieved stardom by pulling the South African float in the Lord Mayor's Show in the City of London.

The Jolly Farmer Inn c. 1930, showing the entrance and the Portsmouth Road and London Road junction. Prior to 1823 it was The Golden Farmer, named after William Davis, a local highwayman who paid his debts in gold. These premises are now the American Discount Golf Shop

One of the large houses typical of those popular in Camberley, c. 1920. This one is Chestnut Lodge; it was in Grand Avenue, next to the recreation ground, which is seen in the foreground. The house has gone, but the more modern replacement retains its name.

This postcard from 1940 was written by a John Carter. He states that he is being evacuated to Market Drayton. This building is now part of Collingwood School, and is next to the Fire Station.

A aerial shot of the same school from about 1935, this time with the London Road running from left to right. The track alongside the school is now Ballard Road.

LONDON ROAD FROM MUNICIPAL OFFICES, CAMBERLEY.

K.99

Morris 8's and Vauxhalls are commonplace in this 1953 scene in the London Road, showing the old Municipal Offices, which now form part of a residential complex. Next door is the Victoria Hotel, which closed a few years later. It could accommodate eight people and had stables for six horses. At one time it had a bowling green at the rear.

It's 1907 and the Municipal Offices have just been built, having been opened the previous year. The building was designed by local architect Mr Poulter, and were built at a cost of £2,339.

Pride of place on this 1955 greetings card is given to a view of the High Street, looking towards the London Road. The house right at the top of the picture is the Staff College.

London Road in 1915. The road stretches towards York Town, with the Municipal Offices the last building on the left. Number 42 – Whites Garage – was where Percy White started his business. My late father commenced working there in 1914 and earned the princely sum of 2/6d. a week. He stayed with Whites until 1979. Whites sold bicycles and used to look after the motor cycles belonging to the officer cadets at the Royal Military College. Later they moved to premises in York Road.

This is St Helen's, probably *c.* 1920. In all probability it was in Heatherdale Road. Today it is called La Paul and is a residential home.

Baldwin Brown Convalescent Home in 1955 was situated off the Upper Chobham Road, and has only recently been demolished to make room for an estate of houses.

Two

York Town
and Frimley Road

When we build, let us think that we build for ever.

John Ruskin, 1819–1900

This early 1904 photo of the London Road is looking towards the Duke of York Hotel. Next to where the couple are standing is the Criterion P.H. Today it is the Treasure Chest, and the name Criterion can still be seen

Closer to the Frimley Road in the same year with the junction clearly visible.

A fine view of the Duke of York Hotel, which was built in 1816 by William Belsher Parfett at a cost of £677 5s. On the opposite corner was Simmonds Bank, which later became Barclays.

The same junction from the opposite direction in 1910. Drew's shop, on the right, produced the two pictures on the opposite page.

London Road. Camberley.

W.H.A.217A.

This scene of the Osnaburgh Parade in 1915 shows the infinite variety of shops available to residents. Shoe shops, jewellers, grocers, and fishmongers are just some of the shops on view. The last shop on the right is now a taxi office. The Parade was named after Frederick, Duke of York, who had the bishopric of Osnaburgh. The Duke of York Hotel also commemorates him.

London Road, 1905, with the Duke of York Hotel just visible on the left. The other buildings, with the exception of the Kings Arms, have now been replaced by office blocks.

About the same time, but a little further towards the Frimley Road. Unfortunately the cart obscures the motor car parked outside the Hotel.

London Road, *c.* 1930. The Crown Hotel, formerly the Bricklayers Arms, is on the right. The town has quite a modern look, with tarmacadam roads and telegraph poles. Only the shop fronts have changed.

Frimley Road and London Road, 1910. On the right, next door to the Duke of York Hotel, is the old Royal Arms public house, which ceased trading in 1907.

An ice cream vendor outside the Duke of York, which now has an impressive covered entrance. This picture was taken in 1938. The premises is now rather neglected, and is boarded up awaiting demolition.

A interior view of the hotel from about 1920.

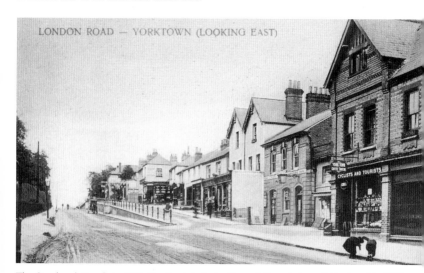

The Osnaburgh Parade in 1907. On the right is the Fox and Hounds inn, which closed in 1925.

38

A pleasant view of the shops in York Town in 1911, which have now been replaced by modern offices. Transport has progressed and outside Drew's is a motor cycle. Before changing its name to York Town in 1931, the area was called New Town, for obvious reasons.

This 1907 view of the London Road shows the York Town School on the left opposite the original Globe, which did not move premises until 1938. The school has now become the Islamic Centre.

More of the shops and the R.M.C. entrance at York Town in 1913.

40

Osnaburgh Parade, looking towards Camberley along the main road, *c.* 1908.

It's 1941, and the Globe has moved to new premises. The London Road is now looking fairly modern with its tarmacadam surface and white lines.

The Odeon Cinema, which became Robins Cinema, opened on 27 August 1932, with a showing of *Jack's the Boy* starring Jack Hulbert and Cicely Courtneidge, and *One Good Turn* with Laurel and Hardy. It was called the Regal in those days and had a pleasant tea room. This photograph dates from about 1940. It has now shut its door, leaving Camberley without a cinema. The most recent plannin application for a lap-dancing club was refused, so its future looks uncertain.

Frimley Road, c. 1920, with a bus approaching. A bus service between Camberley and Aldershot started in 1913.

Frimley Road in 1906, with the entrance to Woodlands on the right. In the distance is the spire of St Michael's Church.

Frimley Road, Camberley.

A little further along the Frimley Road, this time in 1917, with the spire in the distance.

Frimley Park House, Frimley Road, 1950, viewed from the road. It was originally the site of a hunting lodge dating from the early 1600s.

THE CADET TRAINING CENTRE, FRIMLEY PARK

A 1958 aerial view of the house, showing the gardens to the rear. It was built in about 1760 by Sir Henry Tichborne and enlarged at the beginning of this century. Since 1943 it has been owned by the army. It was the W.R.A.C. Staff College from 1951–57 and since 1958 it has been the headquarters of the Cadet Training Centre. At one time it was the home of Captain Charles Raleigh Knight (see picture at the top of page 92).

Krooner Park Parade, c. 1955. Hatto and Son is still there today. Many other traders have gone, but the buildings have not altered.

Three

School Days

I have had playmates, I have had companions,
In my days of childhood, in my joyful school-days,
All, all are gone, the old familiar faces.

Charles Lamb, 1775–1834

Above: The Royal Albert Orphan Asylum, 1950. The building with the clock tower was the main assembly hall, and was only demolished in 1994, having been severely damaged by fire in 1987. The Orphanage is now situated at Reigate, and is called the Royal Alexandra and Albert School, and is most;y residential.

Left: Stan Cooper in 1919 with the forage cap and button up tunic worn by boys. It was a mixed school until 1903, when it was resolved not to admit any more girls.

The Assembly Hall in 1980, which was used as the chapel of the W.R.A.C. until they moved from the premises. The Orphanage opened in 1864 and Queen Victoria was its Patron. The children were not only educated in the 'three Rs', but were also taught a trade or profession to enable them to earn a living when they left the school. It was set in 200 acres of land and included a farm. The grounds are now split by the M3, and the site is now Wellington Park, a modern development of houses.

My father was in this class at Camberley Infants School in 1905. I later attended the same school, when only the staff had changed and the playground had been covered with tarmac. Back row, left to right: Pollard, -?-, Nickleson, Gould, Soan, -?-, Johnson, George Clarke (my father), Allsworth, Swan, Elliott. Second row: Davis, Davis, -?-, Farrow, -?-, -?-, -?-, Pim, Pim, Wallace. Third row. Williams, Flippence, Sandford, Deverell, Smith, Keatley, -?-, Venner, -?-, Crosby. Front row: Armstrong, Mustow, Cocks, -?-, -?-, Pike, -?-.

Park Street railway bridge, 1907, with a tanker engine that had jumped the tracks, toppling down the embankment. The policeman is PC Holdaway.

A 1912 look at the interior of Camberley School.

52

Above: School Lane, 1969, showing both schools on the right. The Infants School opened in 1889 with 44 children. The Primary School was opened in 1897 with the admittance of 123 children. A comparison with today's town centre would be to look up Cambridge Walk by Sainsburys, which is more or less where School Lane was.

Opposite above: Princess Street and Camberley Primary School in School Lane photographed in 1969, before the building of the town centre.

Opposite below: The remains of Cross Street, with Camberley Infants School awaiting its demolition in 1969. In the background is the Camberley Working Men's Club.

The York Town schools in 1913 showing the Infants and the Primary Schools, which both opened in the 1860s. Today they comprise the St Gregorys Catholic School.

France Hill School summer camp in Guernsey, 1955. The fourteen-day trip cost £7 16s. Pictured are David Wells, Graham Simpson, Guy Sutton, Richard Lawrence, Doug Bird, Sidney Mitchell, Ken Waldie, and Mick Mountford. The author is in the front, his feet closest to the camera.

Four

Church and Worship

She came to the village church,
   And sat by a pillar alone,
   An angel watching an urn
Wept over her, carved in stone.

Alfred, Lord Tennyson, 1809–1892

Above: St Michael's Church, York Town, *c.* 1900. The dirt track was the London Road.

Left: St Michael's Church and the churchyard, 1911.

London Road by the Osnaburgh Parade, 1910, and an impressive military cortege slowly makes its way along the road. The small boy on the left, marked with a X, is my late father. Unfortunately he was unable to remember whose funeral it was. Top left is the Globe, and the monumental masons, with the crosses outside, was Mannell and Sons.

St Paul's Church, 1905, at the top of Church Hill. The church was designed by Mr W.D. Caroe in the Swedish style and was completed in 1902.

A 1916 look at St Michael's, this time with the main road stretching towards Blackwater.

A service on the common land in Camberley in 1911.

The same year, with the Bishop of London, in the cloak, taking the service at Church Parade.

Camberley Congregational Church, which was on the corner of Southwell Avenue and Southern Road, in 1935.

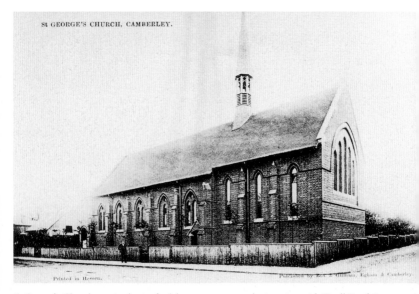

St George's Church was in the road of the same name, at the junction with Knoll Road. It was demolished in about 1968. Like my father I used to be in the choir. This picture is dated 1903.

St Peter's Church, Frimley, in 1907. The present church dates from 1826, although there was a chapel there by 1606. The baptism register dates from 1590, and there is a communion plate from 1586.

An interior photo of St Peter's Church, 1912.

London Road and St Michael's Church, *c.* 1950, before the church yard was altered and cut away, as it is today. In the days before car ownership was so common, the most popular mode of transport, especially locally, was by bus. The largest company was the Aldershot and District Traction Company Limited, or, as it was more commonly referred to, the 'Traco'.

The interior of St Michael's Church in 1920. It was built in 1850, with the tower being added in 1891 as a memorial to Freda Middleton, daughter of the Vicar, the Revd Frederick Middleton. He was Vicar from 1868–1895.

St Paul's Church, 1910, showing the original church, now the church hall, and the present church to the right.

Brompton Sanatorium Chapel, 1980. Building commenced in 1910 and was finally completed in 1925, at a cost of £837. The original plan was to have a building of Bath stone, but owing to money problems this plan had to be abandoned and the design of a wooden building with tiles was agreed. The Chapel was consecrated by the Bishop of Guildford on 21 January 1926.

Five

Royal Military College

There never was a good war, or a bad peace.

Benjamin Franklin, 1706–1790

The York Town entrance to the R.M.A.S. in 1910. The lodge was built in 1831 following a cholera epidemic in the area, to protect the Cadets.

The Terrace, R.M.A.S., with what was known locally as 'Tea Caddy Row', thirteen pairs of cottages built to house the professors, which cost £42,258 in total in 1813.

The Drive and Lake.
RMC Sandhurst. 8920.

The road and boating lake as one enters from the York Town entrance in 1912. This road leads to the front of the College building, which can just be seen between the branches of the tree.

A sunny day by the lake in the attractive grounds in 1912.

The boating lake and the New College in the background. On the left is the boating shed.

The boating lake and island in 1923.

The end of the same lake with the London Road to the right, *c.* 1920

A splendid view of the College, with the Queen Victoria statue looking down on the approaching traffic. The statue was unveiled by The Duke of Connaught on behalf of King Edward VII on 27 July 1904, and was erected by Cadets and others who had connections with the College. Behind the statue is Kings Walk.

The cricket ground is to the right of the main building, and the gymnasium is now the library. This image dates from about 1909.

Library, Pavilion and New Buildings, R.M.C. Camberley.

Another look at the cricket ground, with the library to the left. The building was first used as a library in 1931.

New College in 1948, and the road on the left leads to the Staff College entrance. In the foreground is the Kurnool Mortar, which was formerly at Woolwich. It was found in India in 1839 and bought to its present location in 1946. It weighs just under nine tons and has a bore of 27 inches.

This postcard is dated 1923, and the writer describes Camberley as a pretty place. This shows the steps of the main entrance to the College.

A view of the College across the grassy front, dated 1902.

A picture from the air of the library and cricket ground in the foreground, and New College behind. Beyond are further buildings and pine trees, which show what Camberley must have looked like before development took place.

This photograph of R.M.C. Hospital was taken in 1913 by someone who worked there and sent it to one of their friends. It opened in 1910.

The main building and clock tower of New College in 1939.

A view of the New College, this time showing the other side, taken from the library. New College was built in 1911 and on its completion doubled the size of the R.M.C. Later, in 1862, the Staff College opened, and with it Cambridge Town was built, later to become Camberley in 1877, owing to confusion over wrongly delivered mail.

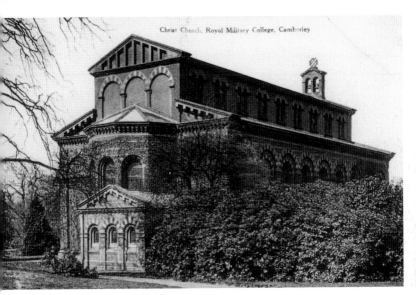

Christ Church, Royal Military College, Camberley

The Christ Church R.M.A.S., 1915, before alterations. The church was built in 1879, and since 1947, after the amalgamation of the R.M.A.S. with Woolwich, it has been the parent church for officers throughout the army. In 1950, new memorial pews and a new organ and screen were added.

Christ Church, Royal Military College, Sandhurst.

Above: A more recent picture, c. 1927.

Left: The interior showing the altar and choir stalls. The windows at the east end were erected to the memory of Colonel F.R. Chesney, a former professor and well-known writer on military subjects.

The Chapel, Royal Military College, Sandhurst. Camberley

amberley, Royal Military College, Memorial to all men.

The Memorial to All Men which stands outside the west door is dedicated to the rank and file of the British Army, who fell in two World Wars. The bronze group was executed by Lady Feodora Gleichen, and the original cast of this group can be found at Monchy le Preux, in France, as a memorial to the 27th Division in the Great War.

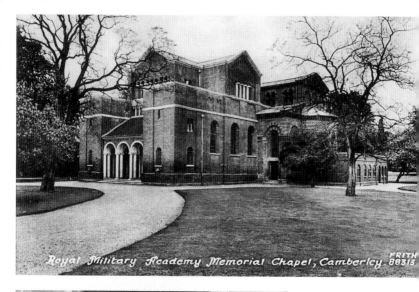

Royal Military Academy Memorial Chapel, Camberley.

FRITH 88315

Above: A further view of the east end, *c.* 1928

Left: The new east end, which was completed in 1937. Inside is a roll, which contains the names of 19,781 Army officers in Britain and the Commonwealth who lost their lives in the Wars. Each is hand written, and the work, by Miss Elizabeth Friedlander, took nearly five years to complete.

Six

Staff College

The 'eathen in 'is blindness must end where 'e began,
But the backbone of the Army is the non commissioned man.

Rudyard Kipling, 1865–1936

Entrance to R.M.C.
Camberley. A.656.

The Staff College entrance, which in 1912 was known as the R.M.C. entrance. The London Road is in the foreground. The trees to the left have not yet given way to the war memorial.

A view of the same entrance, this time from the other way, c. 1950.

An overall look at the entrance in 1960, showing the war memorial which was erected in 1922 at a cost of £433.

The Staff College entrance, 1908, with the coach preparing to leave with its mainly straw-boatered occupants. This was no doubt how officers were met and taken to the railway station.

STAFF COLLEGE ROAD, CAMBERLEY. 512.

A view towards the R.M.C. in 1905 with the bridge over the wishstream, which is the county boundary between Surrey and Berkshire.

The same year and a look at the bridge taken from the boating lake. To the right is now Victory College.

The Staff College in 1907, showing the beech tree planted by Prince Albert in 1860.

The Staff College showing the fine building designed by James Pennethorne, who was a pupil of Nash.

A much later photo, and we can see the additional floor which was added to the building in 1913. The small building to the right is now the N.A.F.F.I. shop. The building was opened in 1862 at a cost of £50,000. On 22 November 1861, Queen Victoria and Prince Albert, who both took a keen interest in the building, drove over from Windsor in the pouring rain to inspect the progress. On his return Albert complained of being tired, and he died of typhoid fever on 14 December in the same year.

Staff College Lake, Camberley (South View)

This lake is directly in front of the entrance to the College, and is more commonly known as the Upper or Fishing Lake. This image dates from about 1920.

The Chinese Bridge, 1909, which was in the woods behind the College. The writer of this postcard complains that since the laurels have been cut down the bridge is not the same.

Seven

People

All the world's a stage
And all the men and women merely players.
They have their exits and their entrances.

William Shakespeare, 1564–1616

Yorkstown Entrance. R. M. Coll.   Sandhurst.

A local tradesman in his cart, and a local woman in her finery outside the York Town entrance to the R.M.C. in 1910.

An army band outside the Christ Church R.M.C., 1908.

Camberley Fire Brigade pictured in 1889 with their Merryweather Pump. The Brigade was formed in May of that year. Their base from 1900 until 1967, before moving to their present location, was in The Avenue. The horses that pulled the pump were borrowed from Mrs Young at the Staff Hotel. Left to right: Chief Officer J. Moss, S. Doman, F. Clarke, H. Lunn, H. Goffe, Second Officer Cottrell, E. Gasby, Engineer J. Mealing. Standing at front: W. Christmas and J. Gaylor.

Charles Raleigh Knight, photographed
c. 1880, lived at Frimley Park and was responsible
for building the first roads in Camberley, including
Park Road, High Street, Park Street, and Crawley and
Church Hill. He also built the Cambridge Hotel.

A sketch of James Cobbett, born in Frimley in 1804, and a
renowned cricket player. He played for Middlesex and was also
lent to Hertfordshire on one occasion, where because of his
tremendous performance the team was called 'Cobbett with
Hertfordshire', and not the other way round. He died in 1842
from consumption, and is buried in Kensal Green Cemetery.

J. Temple Cooke, JP, who lived at Edmonscote, where Ravenscote School in the Old Bisley Road now stands. He was Chairman of the Camberley Court from 1909-25, and was also a Recorder of Southampton.

Alderman A.C. Pain, Chairman of the Camberley Court 1925-27, used to live at St Catherines, St Catherines Road, Frimley. He was also a County Councillor, and in addition to others, was responsible for the setting up of the Frimley and Farnborough Water Company in 1893.

Above: This 1926 photograph is of Mr W. Markham, who had a tobacconist and confectioner shop at 9 High Street.

Left: Two Special Constables. On the left is Percy White, founder of Whites Garage, and on the right is Frank Stallwood, whose Grandfather came to Camberley when the Royal Military College came in 1812. He was a bootmaker by occupation. This image dates from about 1930.

The Princess of Wales, later to become Queen Mary, at the opening of Brompton Sanatorium on Saturday 25 June 1904. She was accompanied by her husband, the Prince of Wales, later to become King George V. The Sanatorium was built for the treatment of consumption (tuberculosis). They also raised their own chickens and pigs, and built a water reservoir at the rear to enable them to deal adequately with any fires that may have occurred. It is now the Ridgewood Centre and is in the Old Bisley Road, Frimley.

This is part of the Camberley and District contribution to the Pageant of Runnymede, which took place at Runnymede from 9–16 June 1934. This shows the Stuart period, and was presided over by the Chairman for Camberley, Lt Colonel J.A.S. Murray, D.S.O. The two Transport Officers were Herman Solomon and Percy White, both garage owners. One of the Masters of the Horse for the whole event was Captain Bertrum Mills, J.P., whose circus had its winter base at Ascot. There were some 6,000 performers, also 2 elephants, 6 donkeys, 100 horses and 4 goats, and they were watched by 90,000 spectators during the 14 performances.

This is George Henry Clarke, my father, pictured at the rear of 42 London Road, shortly after he started work at Whites in 1914. He stayed there for 65 years, and retired in 1979. For his 2/6d. a week in wages he had to work a six-day week, and his last job on a Saturday was to cycle to Eversley to deliver a can of petrol.

St Michael's F.C. in 1958, whose origin was a club of the same name that had its base in The Avenue at Camberley. Back row, left to right: Gordon Herridge, John Knuckey, Jim Clark, Mick Barratt, Ian Rowe. Front row: -?-, Ken Clarke (author), -?- Alan Toogood, Bill Hayward, Brian Clay.

Kate Ward, or 'Camberley Kate' as she became known after media coverage of her hobby of looking after stray dogs in the area. She lived in London Road, York Town, with her dogs and could regularly be seen walking them. She died in 1979 at the age of 84.

St Michael's Club outside their building in The Avenue in 1923. The Club was formed in 1884 and their first base was in the London Road. The man standing in the back of the charabanc with a trilby hat is my late father.

These German prisoners are marching from Frimley Station to Frith Hill Camp, which was on the common opposite what is now the Ridgewood Centre in the Old Bisley Road. They are pictured here in Station Approach in 1916 (see page 122).

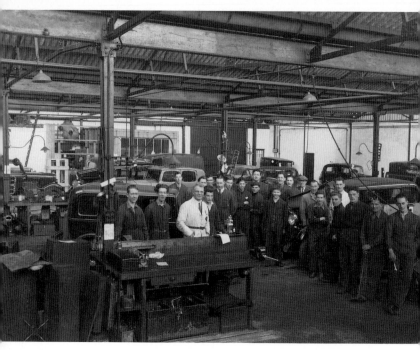

Inside Whites Crash Shop, York Road, in 1938. It certainly was a busy place in those days judging by the number of staff in view. The Foreman, in the white coat, is Tommy Topliffe, and others include Tom Streeter, Ray Balcombe, Nobby Hall, Bill Bartlett, George Hemsley and Curly Carter.

Eight

Sport and Leisure-time

For when the One Great Scorer comes
To write against your name,
He writes not that you won or lost,
But how you played the game.

Grantland Rice, 1880–1954

The Aspen Tree with Henry Clarke, my grandfather, leaning against the door with his arms folded. He was licencee there from 1907 until its closure in 1925. It was in the London Road, just before the Upper Charles Street junction. Beer was 2d. a pint and cigarettes were 1s. for 20. It could accommodate four people and two horses.

Camberley Recreation Ground in 1957, where now the Arena Leisure Centre now stands.

Camberley, Barossa, Old Dean Common.

How much of Camberley looked in 1912, when walking on the common was a healthy pastime. During the 1948 Olympic Games, some of the horseriding events took place on the Common.

Camberley Working Men's Club in 1936, with the pump of Solomons Garage visible to the left. The first Club building was destroyed by fire on 2 November 1929.

Camberley Heath, Golf Links Club House.

The Club House at Camberley Heath Golf Club, recently pulled down. It was built in 1913 and cost £4,000. The first ball was struck on 1 January 1914 by Prince Christian of Schlesswig-Holstein.

Barossa Golf Club.
Camberley.   A. 679.

A 1919 look at Barossa Golf Club, which was off King's Ride and consisted of a nine-hole course. It was owned by John Donald Craig, who died in 1909, after which the Club was taken over by his son W.D. Craig. Today, the Club has disappeared and the site is used by the Colleges as playing fields. During the war it was part of Reynolds Farm.

The Blue Pool, 1956, with the London Road in the foreground. The site has now become the Manor House, a block of superior flats, and the pool has gone.

The High Street and London Road, 1953, and the arrival of a circus procession making its way to the Recreation Ground.

THE BLUE POOL, CAMBERLEY.

37575

The Blue Pool, 1944, with a view looking towards the main road. The pool itself was 200 feet long and 50 feet wide, and it was surrounded by trees with a grassy bank on one side. There was a small children's pool to the right. It opened in 1934 under private ownership and was bought by the Council in 1973, but after problems with leaks it was decided to close it and in 1977 the town lost an attractive asset.

Surrey Junior Cup Final.
WOKING, 1908

Camberley & Yorktown.

J. Shaw. H. Griffiths, D. Brown.
A. Knapton. (Capt.) W. King. J. Nolan.
N. Baldwin, D. Sparvell. E. Rideout J. Hunt. T. Milton

4th Camberley Cubs marching into the York Town gate of the R.M.A.S. on St George's Day, 1951, with the Duke of York Hotel in the background. At the head is the indomitable Mrs Houghton, who did much work for the Pack. Included in the picture are Tub Hawkins, Roger Wallis, Michael Elkins, and the author can be seen in the second row, on the right.

Opposite above: Camberley and York Town lost to Kingston 2–0 in the Final. T. Milton, a postman, was a prisoner of war and upon his release in 1919 he returned home, but died in 1929 at the age of 42, due, it was reported, to his suffering as a prisoner in Germany.

Opposite below: The neatly-kept gardens at the Recreation Ground, 1929.

Whites Football Team, 1952. Back row (left to right): Mick James, Mick Sargent, J. Ahern, R. Weston, H. Mullard, Jock Green, K. Erskine, M. Beck. Seated: Colin Upton, M. McEvine, Eddy Harris, Eric\ Piper, M. Hanscombe.

Camberley Football Club pictured in 1909, when they played at Southwell Park, now part of the town car parks. Included in the team are: Knapton, Bowdery, Shaw, Daborn, Brown, Wills, Rumble, Nolan, Baldwin, Hunt, Baston, and Milne.

Camberley Heath, Golf Links

A 1924 look at the Links at Camberley Heath Golf Club. The writer of this postcard has marked where her house is.

The Foresters Arms, Bagshot, with Lawrence Reynolds, my mother's father, outside. He was licencee until 1931. He joined the Grenadier Guards in 1899, and transferred to the Irish Guards in 1900. At Pirbright he claims he was the Irish Guardsman for a fortnight, until some other soldiers arrived to join the new formation. He fought at Omdurman in 1898 and captured a young Boer commando, Malan, who later became Prime Minister for the country.

St Michael's Cricket Team in 1910, with Tom Mounce, third from left in the second row.
Included in the picture is G. Cox. The author, in his youth, also played cricket for St Micheals,
in the late 1950s and early '60s.

The 1920 Camberley Police Tug of War Team. Back row, second from the left, is the writer of
this postcard, PC 141 Freddy Bicknell, and two places from him is Bob Hersey.

Camberley Railway Station, 1931, with the Micheline Train. This was an experimental train which ran on rubber tyres, similar to the Metro in Paris. It ran from Ascot to Alton twice a day, and could hold 24 passengers as well as their luggage. It could reach speeds of 60 mph and did 12 miles to the gallon on its petrol engine. One of the main reasons why it did not catch on was that the rubber tyres could not break the fog detonators put on the track in fog to warn drivers of a hazard.

Nine

Around Camberley

*'Camberley, one of the most attractive and beautiful residential centres
to be found within the confines of the pine district.'*

London and South Western Railway Guide, 1902

Blackwater Bridge, 1927, with the ford to the left which was the crossing place prior to the first bridge being built in 1805–6. This present bridge dates from 1930.

London Road, Blackwater, in 1908. The White Hart Hotel is the large building at the end of the road.

Blackwater Station, 1909, with the level crossing in the background. The station was opened in 1848 and was originally known as Blackwater and York Town. It was used a lot by officer cadets from the College. The building shown was a replacement for the original one.

London Road, Blackwater, with a view towards the bridge. On the left is the Old Manor Cafe, which used to be the Old Manor House, where my late mother worked in service. This is a 1968 photograph, with Camberley in the background.

Blackwater, with the White Hart on the right, in 1906. Further along is the Royal Swan. The White Hart has been replaced by a block of shops and offices.

A troop of soldiers marching across Blackwater Level Crossing, c. 1913.

The Priors Kitchen, Frimley High Street, 1960, which disappeared in 1964 to become Station Parade. At one time it was a night club, and during the First World War it was used as a military hospital. Colonel Faithful and Colonel Fitzroy-Somerset were some of the other previous occupants.

The Grove, Frimley, in 1935, with the Chobham Road to the right and the Portsmouth Road on the left. Just out of sight is the old pound, where stray animals were tethered until their owners claimed them after paying a fine.

Frimley Cottage Hospital, 1920, with the King Edward VII Wing to the left, which was added in 1911. The Hospital was built in 1909. Today it is the Children's Centre.

German Prisoners Compound, Frith Hill, Frimley. W.H.A.9101.

During the First World War it was deemed necessary to open a concentration camp to house German prisoners, and opposite the then Brompton Hospital was a tented camp which housed upwards of 2,000 men. At weekends, many local residents went there to view the enemy. Some prisoners died there, and others escaped – but they were soon recaptured.

High Street, Frimley, in 1908, with two postmen outside the Post Office. At the junction with the Portsmouth Road, behind the trees would be a lodge to Frimley Park, since demolished.

A 1939 photograph of the Surrey Border and Camberley Railway, which ran from near Frimley Station to the rear of what is now Moorlands Road, a distance of nearly two miles. It was opened in 1938 by Graham Moffat, who appeared in *Oh Mr Porter* with Will Hay. The Railway began as the Foxhills Miniature Railway which was run by a Mr. H.C.S. Bullock in 1934. He went into partnership with a Mr A.D. Kinloch, a merchant banker, and it became the Farnborough Miniature Railway. The line was extended and the name changed again, but with the outbreak of war it closed on 3 September 1939, and with it the area lost an interesting local amenity.

Frimley High Street, 1960, a view taken from the White Hart. The Somerfield store is now to the right, and the houses have been replaced by shops. Up until this time Frimley was a small village, unlike today, when its population is greater than that of Camberley.

The Watchetts, which was at the end of Watchetts Drive and lived in by 'Squire' H.J.B. Hollings, D.L., J.P., He was also, in 1913, President of the Camberley Fire Brigade. The house and gardens have since been built on and Verran Road is now to the right. This photograph dates from about 1956.

Manor Farm, Frimley, in 1959. It was situated off the Frimley Green Road on the right, just past where Johnson Wax is.

Harvest time in 1944, on land next to where Frimley Green Recreation Ground is. In the photograph is a young Dusty Miller and some of his friends.

Frimley High Street c. 1950, and the old Blacksmiths Cottage is being demolished. It was on the same side of the road as the Railway Arms.

126

The Manor House, Frimley, in June 1956. The house was opposite St Peter's Church, and was lived in at that time by the Cotterills. During the early 1900s, the Lord of the Manor was Mr J.F. Burrell, who has had a road named in his memory. The house was demolished in the 1960s and replaced by Apex Drive, a series of blocks of modern houses of an unusual design.

Left: Frimley Green Road in 1944, and the tank is being driven in the direction of Frimley Green. It is almost outside the Frimley Police Office.

Below: High Street, Frimley, 1939, with Maybury House to the left. Dr Augustus Maybury was resident at one time, and before that it was called Cedar House. Up until a few years ago it was the Frimley Post Office.